101 FAVORITE BIBLE VERSES
For Women

Publications International, Ltd.

Contributing writers: Cecil Cole, Elaine Wright Colvin, Elaine Creasman, Christine Dallman, Janice Deal, June Eaton, Lain Chroust Ehmann, Margaret Anne Huffman, Marie D. Jones, Wallis C. Metts, Carol Smith, Natalie Walker Whitlock, Gary Wilde

Cover and interior art: Shutterstock.com

Louis Weber, CEO
Publications International, Ltd.
8140 Lehigh Avenue
Morton Grove, IL 60053

ISBN: 978-1-68022-756-7

Manufactured in China.

8 7 6 5 4 3 2 1

The Bible has been a source of inspiration, strength, courage, contemplation, and spiritual wisdom for millions of people throughout the timeline of our current era. People have turned to it for comfort in times of need, and they have relied on it to give them direction in their life. From the book of Psalms of the Old Testament to the Gospels of the New Testament, the Bible provides an everlasting refuge for when you have no place to go.

101 Favorite Bible Verses for Women is filled with pertinent scriptures and prayers that address all of the complicated facets of the spiritual lives of women, from how to be a devoted follower of Christ to a loving member of a family. This book contains devotions, prayers, and words of wisdom that will lead you down the path of unfaltering faith, giving you the patience, courage, and resilience to do the work of God. Be devoted, be faithful, and be good with the help of *101 Favorite Bible Verses for Women*.

Be strong and of a good courage, fear not, nor be afraid of them: for the Lord thy God, he it is that doth go with thee; he will not fail thee, nor forsake thee.

—Deuteronomy 31:6

*T*he path of love is never easy. Yet it is in the ups and downs, the times of trouble and need, that together you forge a bond strong enough to withstand whatever the road ahead may bring.

For thou art my lamp, O Lord:
and the Lord will lighten my darkness.

—2 Samuel 22:29

*T*here are three kinds of people in the world: those who give off light, those who give off dark shadows, and those who give off nothing. Choose to be a giver of light, a bearer of hope, a bringer of faith. For only light can dispel the darkness, and only light can brighten deadened places and bring them back to life. **"Do not hide your light under a bushel,"** Jesus admonished us. We were not meant to cower fearfully amid the shadows or to huddle in dark corners undetected. We were meant to go forth into the world and shine.

Strengthen ye the weak hands,
and confirm the feeble knees.

—Isaiah 35:3

*N*ever underestimate the power of a loving touch.

With him is strength and wisdom:
the deceived and the deceiver are his.

—Job 12:13

Aim high, believing that God has great things in store for us as mothers and for our families. Never mind nay-sayers and roadblocks, for we are **guided by God.**

For the gifts and calling of God
are without repentance.

—Romans 11:29

After making plans to go hiking with friends, I remembered my boots were a half size too small. My budget, however, was telling me that new footwear was out of the question. Without much hope, I decided to visit a sporting-goods store. As I drove there, I spotted a thrift store and felt a strong impulse to stop in. "God, please let there be a good pair of hiking boots in my size here," I prayed. Scanning the rows of shoes, I found only one pair of authentic hiking boots, and they were in new condition. But would they fit? I fumbled to find the sizing information. When I read it, I wanted to let out a whoop, but instead I whispered, "Thank you, God!" Then, handing the cashier a mere eight dollars and some change, I couldn't help but say **"Thank you"** again.

But they that wait upon the Lord shall renew their strength; they shall mount up with wings as eagles; they shall run, and not be weary; and they shall walk, and not faint.

—Isaiah 40:31

As storm clouds gathered, Father, I used to run for cover, panicked and picking a favorite escape. None of them worked for long, Dear God, and none of them kept me safe. No more running then. I see it clearly now: Wherever I am standing is a special place, under the shadow of your sheltering wing.

The Lord shall preserve thy going out and thy coming
in from this time forth, and even for evermore.

—Psalm 121:8

I recently retired after almost forty years of teaching. As much as I enjoyed my job, I am reveling in the opportunities this new chapter affords. I have always loved travel, and for many years dreamed of visiting Europe. My gift to myself this next year is a month-long tour through France and Italy. While I am excited, I am also a little anxious because I'll be traveling solo. I have never been away from home for so long. Dear God, thank you for this opportunity. Please bless my travels. Please guide and protect me as I visit new places, meet new people, and broaden my horizons. May I make the most of this journey.

Now therefore ye are no more strangers
and foreigners, but fellow citizens with the saints,
and of the household of God.

—*Ephesians 2:19*

Community enriches us, granting us a sense of belonging, mutual support, and opportunities to exchange ideas and knowledge. But in today's transient culture, people move all the time, often because of job opportunities or changes. A move to a new place can be an exciting opportunity, of course. But uprooting from a familiar place, with its reassuring ties, can be unsettling. You had found someone who cut your hair just right; you knew who to call when the pipe under the sink sprouted a leak. Perhaps most importantly, you had a network of friends and loved ones who helped you feel at home in the world. It takes time to re-establish a sense of community after a move, but God is present to help us on the journey. In an unfamiliar place, have faith that you will find your people.

I can do all things through Christ
which strengtheneth me.

—Philippians 4:13

I t is easy to have faith when things are going well, when the bills are paid and everyone is happy and in good health. But blessed is the person who has steadfast and unmoving faith when everything is going wrong. That's when faith is most needed—and least employed. If a person can suspend all intellectual judgment, look beyond the illusion of negative appearances, and believe in a Higher Power at work behind the scenes, faith will begin to move mountains, and positive solutions will appear. By putting the mighty power to work, faith will begin to work some **mighty powerful miracles** in your life.

Yea, though I walk through the valley of the shadow of death, I will fear no evil: for thou art with me; thy rod and thy staff they comfort me.

—Psalm 23:4

*T*his past year has been a challenging one. My son Gary, who began his freshman year at university in the fall, became overwhelmed by his course work, and his physical and emotional health suffered. After flunking several of his first-semester classes, he recently returned home. My husband and I are doing our best to support him emotionally, and we have talked, as a family, about Gary getting a job and earning some extra money while he regroups. We've also talked about him taking some classes at the local community college. But he is very depressed and finding it difficult to make decisions, and I myself am deeply saddened by his unhappiness and confusion. Dear Lord, your loving presence provides solace. Please comfort Gary. Please fill my heart, and help my husband and me to know how to encourage our son and help him work through this difficult chapter.

Fear thou not; for I am with thee: be not dismayed;
for I am thy God: I will strengthen thee; yea, I will
help thee; yea, I will uphold thee with the right hand
of my righteousness.

—Isaiah 41:109

My mom died of cancer when I was still in college. She was diagnosed with a brain tumor in the spring and was gone before Christmas. My dad was devastated and in his grief, withdrew from the world; he could not be there for us kids to lean on emotionally. It was a very difficult time in my life. What got me through was the support I received at the church in my college town. In what was probably the loneliest time in my life, I was nevertheless surrounded by love. Various members of the congregation invited me over for home-cooked meals or pizza-and-movie nights. These folks encouraged me that God was still there, and through their loving actions, I experienced God's grace. **God is with us even when we feel alone.**

Let your conversation be without covetousness; and be content with such things as ye have: for he hath said, I will never leave thee, nor forsake thee.

—Hebrews 13:5

My husband and I attended a party the other night, and the subject of real estate came up. I love our modest home. We raised our kids here, and we've always been comfortable. But when conversation turned to what makes a house "sellable," I became embarrassed. We don't have granite countertops in our kitchen, and the bathrooms, while bright, have outdated fixtures. I came home feeling jealous and uneasy; a spirit of materialism briefly made me see our cozy home in a less flattering light. When I woke the next morning, though, refreshed by sleep, my husband and I enjoyed our coffee while watching the birds from our breakfast nook. I looked around our little house and felt joy. God, you have graced our home with your love. May I not allow materialism to distract me or create anxiety; may I be grateful for the **true blessings** in my life.

God is in the midst of her; she shall not be moved:
God shall help her, and that right early.

—Psalm 46:5

I recently changed jobs. For many years, I'd worked in a doctor's office, and for most of the time, the pros of that situation outweighed the cons. I enjoyed flexible hours—a godsend when my elderly mother grew ill and needed more help. But my boss was never supportive and the pay was not ideal. When my mom passed away last year, I decided to look for a different position, and almost immediately found a new job. I am excited about this next chapter, but change can also be hard. During these first weeks at work, the learning curve has been steep and some nights I am tired and stressed. Dear God, please live in my heart and help me to remain steadfast as I seek to learn, grow, and improve my situation and myself. Please remind me, on the days when my spirit flags, that **you are always there.**

Casting all your care upon him;
for he careth for you.

—1 Peter 5:7

I am the single mom of two teens. The last year has been challenging for me as a parent. My daughter has had a hard time adjusting to the rigors of high school academics, and my son has been testing boundaries when it comes to curfews and expectations at home. Some nights I am troubled by insomnia, and then the next day, I have a shorter fuse. Tempers flare. Dear Lord, please help me to remember that you are there for me. **You are the answer to my anxiety.** Help me to parent with wisdom and rely on you, even when I feel stressed and uncertain.

Have not I commanded thee? Be strong and of a
good courage; be not afraid, neither be thou dismayed:
for the Lord thy God is with thee whithersoever
thou goest.

—*Joshua 1:9*

Dear Lord, my daughter's school life has been miserable lately. For the past four years, she and two other girls have been inseparable. Birthday parties, sleepovers, movie dates: when two of them gather, it's been a given that the third will be invited to join. We've even vacationed with the other girls' families! But this year, something changed: a new girl joined the group, and my daughter has started to feel marginalized. Last week, the other three went shopping and forgot to invite her. When she went to a sleepover, the other girls had a series of private jokes to which my daughter wasn't privy. My heart bleeds for her, and sometimes I have a hard time masking my own anger at the situation. God, please help me to remain strong so that I can be there for my girl; may I help my daughter navigate these difficulties with grace.

By faith Moses, when he was born, was hid three months of his parents, because they saw he was a proper child; and they were not afraid of the king's commandment.

—Hebrews 11:23

My husband and I have three children under the age of ten. We love being parents, even as we understand that parenting can entail sacrifice. This came home to us recently when my husband declined an opportunity for a promotion. Though the job sounded interesting, it meant that he would be traveling three weeks out of every four. We have decided our priority, right now, is for both of us to hold jobs where we can be consistently home and together as a family. The job offer was good, but the timing was not. Though these decisions can be difficult, God reminds us to sacrifice happily for our children. Even if we sometimes have to defer our own gratification, seeing our children thrive is a blessing.

They that sow in tears shall reap in joy.

—*Psalm 126:5*

I'm an emergency-room nurse and love my job, which can be by turns intense, interesting, and challenging. No two days are alike, though much of the time I am invited to think on my feet. I do like that aspect of the job. But lately, the ER has been so busy that by shift's end I find myself exhausted, both mentally and physically. I must remember that what I do has value, and these things run in cycles. I've worked long enough to understand that the pace will eventually settle, at least temporarily, and that I mustn't let a hard day of work get me down. Dear God, help me to take the long view. Remind me on the days when my spirits and energy are low, that ultimately **things always get better.**

Not that I speak in respect of want: for I have learned, in whatsoever state I am, therewith to be content.

—*Philippians 4:11*

*H*uman beings are the only creatures that strive to be something they are not. Perhaps we should take a lesson from the birds of the sky, who never ache to be anything other than creatures able to fly at will upon a lifting breeze. Or we should learn from the fish of the sea, who don't doubt their own ability to glide through blue waters dappled with sunlight. Or maybe we should spend some time watching wild horses thunder over the open plains, and we would see that not once do they stop to wish they were anything more than what God made them: **glorious, beautiful, and free.**

Glory and honour are in his presence;
strength and gladness are in his place.

—*1 Chronicles 16:27*

When we think of integrity, we think of someone who is honorable and trustworthy—a person who keeps their word and guards their reputation. To be called a woman of integrity is a high compliment. Such a person knows the difference between right and wrong and diligently pursues doing right, no matter what the obstacles. Jesus provides the best example of a person of integrity; he was not swayed by outer influences but lived a life above reproach. Integrity comes not just from the pursuit of right living, but the pursuit of God, which leads to right living.

One of the Hebrew names for God is Jehovah Jireh (JY-rah). Besides having a nice ring to it, its meaning, **"God, our provider,"** is one worth remembering. In life, we may experience times of abundance and also times when we struggle to make ends meet. In any situation, God asks us to trust and honor him as Jehovah Jireh, the God who provides all that we truly need.

Nor height, nor depth, nor any other creature,
shall be able to separate us from the love of God,
which is in Christ Jesus our Lord.

—Romans 8:39

No matter how deep a rut we dig ourselves into, the arms of God are long
enough to lift us up into a newer life free
from struggle. No matter how dark a
tunnel we crawl into, **the love of God** is
strong enough to reach in and guide us
toward a brighter life, free from fear.

*But seek ye first the kingdom of God,
and his righteousness; and all these things
shall be added unto you.*

—*Matthew 6:33*

*T*here is no denying the pleasure of creature comforts. Last year, my husband and I decided to take the plunge and have central air conditioning installed in our old home. Every hot day this summer, I have reveled in returning to a blast of cool air when I get home; on some level, the air conditioning has made my life better. But as much as I appreciate it, I must remember not to be distracted by or consumed by physical comforts to the extent that I neglect my spiritual welfare. Dear God, thank you for air conditioning—it is good to feel good! But may I always be cognizant of well-being on the inside as well as the outside; may my focus on the everlasting rewards of your kingdom be unswerving.

He hath made his wonderful works to be remembered:
the Lord is gracious and full of compassion.

—Psalm 111:4

*T*o have talent and not use it is to ignore the calling of a higher voice. To be given gifts and not share them is to nullify the moving of the spirit through the soul as it seeks to be made manifest in the outer world. We are given our light to let it shine, not to hide it from others for fear of drawing attention. For when we shine, we allow others to do so as well. God did not make stars in order to keep them from glowing in the night sky, nor did he make birds in order to keep them grounded. When we open our storehouse of talents and treasures, the whole world benefits and is made brighter.

And when ye stand praying, forgive,
if ye have ought against any: that your Father also
which is in heaven may forgive you your trespasses.

—Mark 11:25

God **prefers** that we make an effort, even if we should initially fail. He will eagerly forgive our mistakes in the hope that we will learn and grow from them.

*L*ove and forgiveness
walk hand in hand.
Our relationships with
God and others are inter-
twined in this dynamic.

God, I pray for the strength and the wisdom to know what to do in this situation. I pray for enough love to forgive this person for the pain they have caused me and to forgive myself for the ill will I have harbored against this person. Help me be a truly forgiving person so that the weight of resentment may be lifted from my shoulders. **Amen.**

And be ye kind one to another, tenderhearted, forgiving one another, even as God for Christ's sake hath forgiven you.

—Ephesians 4:32

*T*o find love, we think we must first find the courage to take a big chance by risking our heart to another; yet it's only then that we discover it's in the very act of offering ourselves that love is found.

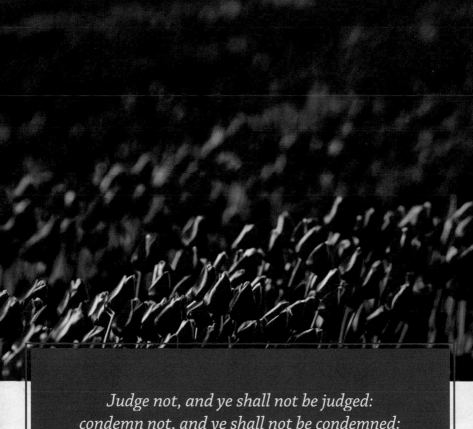

Judge not, and ye shall not be judged:
condemn not, and ye shall not be condemned:
forgive, and ye shall be forgiven. Give, and it shall be
given unto you; good measure, pressed down,
and shaken together, and running over, shall men give
into your bosom. For with the same measure that ye
mete withal it shall be measured to you again.

—Luke 6:37–38

We all have something to offer: time, money, expertise. God exhorts us to give generously; in his infinite wisdom, he understands that when we give, we're not just helping others (worthy in and of itself), but we also help ourselves. Studies have shown that generosity helps to manage personal stress, and have linked unselfishness and giving with a general sense of life satisfaction and a lower risk of early death. When we reach outside ourselves, we connect with others. God wants that connection, that sense of purpose and happiness, for each of us. Dear Lord, help us to connect with our best selves; help us to be generous givers.

And my soul shall be joyful in the Lord:
it shall rejoice in his salvation.

—Psalm 35:9

O Holy Creator, who hath bound together heaven and earth, let me walk through your kingdom comforted and protected by the warm rays of your love. Let me be healed as I stand basking in the divine light of your presence, where strength and hope and joy are found. Let me sit at rest in the valley of your peace, surrounded by the fortress of your **loving care.**

When we think of joy, we often think of things that are near new—a new day, a new baby, a new love, a new beginning, the promise of a new home with God in heaven. Rejoicing in these things originates with having joy in the God who makes all things new. Rather than relying on earthly pleasures to provide happiness, the scriptures command that we rejoice in God and in each new day he brings. Joy is a celebration of the heart that goes beyond circumstances to the very foundation of joy—**the knowledge that we are loved by God.**

Thus speaketh the Lord of hosts, saying,
Execute true judgment, and shew mercy and
compassions every man to his brother.

—*Zechariah 7:9*

We live in an information society. Daily, we are bombarded with news. Our phones, televisions, and laptops keep us breathlessly apprised of the latest events. It is good to be informed, and technology is a gift. But an adverse effect of the all-information-all-the-time mentality is that it numbs the senses. "Another earthquake?" we shrug. "Another tragedy?" It can be an effort to dig deep and access caring, and yet compassion is a godly virtue. God wants us to experience concern for the sufferings of others. Dear Lord, help us to strike a balance in our information intake so that we retain compassion for those in need. **May we never become callous to others' misfortune.**

If ye forsake the Lord, and serve strange gods,
then he will turn and do you hurt, and consume you,
after that he hath done you good.

—Joshua 24:20

When we fill our days with the noisy blur of constant activity, we miss the gifts and blessings of God. Only by purposely taking the time to do nothing can we cultivate the inner wisdom and guidance we seek. It's **in the quiet** that we renew our connection to God. He is our source of inspiration, energy, and enthusiasm. Silence is more than golden. It's essential to a life following his path.

*I*t doesn't matter if we can't see angels. Our ability to feel their silent, supportive presence is a testament to **our faith**.

Thou hast also given me the shield of thy salvation: and thy gentleness hath made me great.

—2 Samuel 22:3

Dear God, no one understands my suffering, but you do, for you know my heart **even better than I do.** Help me to walk through this dark valley of my pain and guide me back to the light of truth. I know that I am precious, but I don't feel that way right now. Help me see the reality of who I am—the magnificent creation you intended me to be. Amen.

Truly my soul waiteth upon God:
from him cometh my salvation.

—*Psalm 62:1*

*T*urn over your problems to God, and he will orchestrate the best outcome.

God, please help me to accept your itinerary for my life's journey **no matter where it brings me.** I will wait for you to decide when I should return to your home. Amen.

Thou hast granted me life and favour,
and thy visitation hath preserved my spirit.

—Job 10:12

Spirit, carry me like a feather upon the current to a place of serenity. Let the waters flow over me like a cleansing balm. Set me upon the dry place, where life begins anew. Spirit, carry me like a feather back home again.

*I*n the midst of the darkness that threatens to overwhelm us lies a pinpoint of light, a persistent flicker that guides us through the pain and fear, through the hopelessness and despair, to a place of peace and healing on the other side. This is **God's Spirit,** leading us back home like the lighthouse beacon that directs the ships through the fog to the safety of the harbor.

O love the Lord, all ye his saints:
for the Lord preserveth the faithful,
and plentifully rewardeth the proud doer.

—*Psalm 31:23*

*L*ord, I'm glad that **the more I give, you give.** Reward me for the risks I take on your behalf. Amen.

God recognizes and rewards faithful work.

Let us draw near with a true heart in full assurance of faith, having our hearts sprinkled from an evil conscience, and our bodies washed with pure water.

—*Hebrews 10:22*

When will the rain let up, Lord?
Oh, soon: may your presence be to me as
cleansing droplets of mercy, these clouds
only filtering in glorious gold and purple
the blazing rays of your grace.

Trust in the Lord with all thine heart; and lean not unto thine own understanding. In all thy ways acknowledge him, and he shall direct thy paths.

—*Proverbs 3:5–6*

*T*hink of each problem you encounter as nothing more than a challenging reminder from God to think a little higher and reach a little further. When met with a difficult situation along the road of life, greet it, acknowledge it, and move past it. Then you will be able to continue on your journey a little stronger, a little wiser.

The Lord hath heard my supplication;
the Lord will receive my prayer.

—Psalm 6:9

*I*n silence I kneel in your presence—
bow my heart to your wisdom and lift my
hands for your mercy. And open my soul
to the great gift: **I am already held in
your arms.**

For whatsoever is born of God overcometh the world:
and this is the victory that overcometh the world,
even our faith.

—1 John 5:4

*T*he creative power within is your power to overcome any obstacle and break through any binding walls that keep you from your dreams. This power was given to you by the greatest of all creators, the One who created you, God. Just look around at the amazing beauty and diversity of the world you live in, and you will **never again doubt** that God supports your creative endeavors.

A strong spirit can **overcome** even the weakest flesh.

Surely goodness and mercy shall follow me all the days of my life: and I will dwell in the house of the Lord forever.

—*Psalm 23:6*

I am still moving, God, through storms. By your grace—over rough country, you have carried me; amidst pounding waves, you have held me; beyond the horizon of my longings, you have shown me your purposes. Even in this small room, sitting still, I am moving, God. **Closer.**

And not only so, but we glory in tribulations also: knowing that tribulation worketh patience.

—Romans 5:3

As a parent, what I wish for my daughter, Anne, is an easy path. When she struggles with her studies or experiences conflicts with friends, my heart aches. I know, however, that no one can be shielded from pain indefinitely, and that it is adversity as well as our joys and successes that shape us. My grandfather used to say that misfortune can build character, and I see that in my daughter. Challenges have shown her that she possesses an inner steel, even as they've demanded she develop patience and compassion. Dear Lord, help me to guide Anne so that she might meet hardship with strength, patience, and grace. May adversity help her to grow as a person.

For where your treasure is,
there will your heart be also.

—Matthew 6:21

*T*rue love is surrendering to the dictates of my healed heart and giving my all, no matter what the risk, no matter what the cost.

She stretcheth out her hand to the poor;
yea, she reacheth forth her hands to the needy.

—*Proverbs 31:20*

My husband and I work hard, but some months money is tight. We have become adept at cutting costs, and although we will never be what our culture considers wealthy, I am grateful that we have what we need. The other day, I read about the devastating flooding in Louisiana, and was reminded of how generosity can manifest itself in different ways. While we can donate a small amount of cash, I also, perhaps more crucially, can devote some of my time to volunteer efforts. I am healthy and can even donate blood. God, I am blessed in so many ways; please help me to remember the importance of generosity, and how it can take many forms.

> *Trust in the Lord, and do good; so shalt thou dwell in the land, and verily thou shalt be fed.*
>
> —Psalm 37:3

*F*aith is a commodity that cannot be purchased, traded, or sold. It is a treasure that cannot be claimed and put on display in a museum. It is a richness no amount of money can compare to. When you have faith, you have a power that can change night into day, move mountains, calm stormy seas. When you have faith, you can fall over and over again, only to get up each time more determined than ever to succeed, and you will succeed. For faith **is God in action,** and faith is available to anyone—rich, poor, young, or old—as long as you believe.

Sing, O heavens; and be joyful, O earth;
and break forth into singing, O mountains:
for the Lord hath comforted his people,
and will have mercy upon his afflicted.

—*Isaiah 49:13*

Mercy is not something we need beg of you, O God, for your pleasure is to love us. Mercy, grace, and love are always available to us, Lord, for you are always available to us. **Mercy is one of the great gifts of God.**

God knows that as hard as we may try, there are times when we will make human mistakes. Even so, if we trust in him and ask his forgiveness, he will bless us with mercy and peace.

*My little children, let us not love in word,
neither in tongue; but in deed and in truth.*

—1 John 3:1

Whom you choose to love and how you demonstrate your commitment says **more about you** than it does about the object of your affection.

Thou lovest righteousness, and hatest wickedness:
therefore God, thy God, hath anointed thee with the
oil of gladness above thy fellows.

—Psalm 45:7

*H*elp me, God, to see that you gave your love in such a way that even the most wicked person can repent and find new life in your grace and mercy; indeed, that your love calls **even the worst sinners** to become your children. You created each person with a specific purpose to serve in this world. Help me, Lord, to pray that each person will turn away from evil, turn to you, and become your devoted servant. Amen.

Comfort ye, comfort ye my people, saith your God.

—Isaiah 40:1

God, help me to accept the help I need and to give up my stubborn need to control the outcome of every situation. Show me that sometimes my will is not always the best and that sometimes you send us healing angels **in the form of other humans.** Thank you. Amen.

*L*ord, thank you for bringing others into our lives to **help us heal.** We appreciate how much they aid us. Please remind us to thank them for reaching out to us. Thank you for extending your love to us through them. Amen.

He hath filled the hungry with good things;
and the rich he hath sent empty away.

—Luke 1:53

*T*here is a difference between wishing that something was so and having faith that it will be. Wishing implies an attitude of hope based on fantasy and daydreams. Faith implies an attitude of belief based upon reality and intentions. You can wish for a thing all you want, but until you have **complete faith** that it can—and will—be yours, it will be just a wish.

Behold, how good and how pleasant it is for brethren to dwell together in unity!

—Psalm 133:1

I am feeling my way in this darkness, God, and it seems I'm going in circles. Yet you have reminded me—quietly, just now—that encircled by your love with every move in any direction I go. I travel no closer to you—nor further—because I am already centered within you.

The curse of the Lord is in the house of the wicked:
but he blesseth the habitation of the just.

—Proverbs 3:33

God, I couldn't help noticing all the loveliness you placed in the world today! This morning I witnessed a sunrise that made my heart beat faster. Then, later, I watched a father gently help his child across a busy parking lot; his tenderness was much like yours. While inside a department store, I spied an elderly couple sitting on a bench. I could hear the man cracking jokes; their laughter lifted my spirits. Then early this evening, I walked by a woman tending her flowerbed; she took great pleasure in her work, and her garden was breathtaking. Later, I talked with a friend who is helping some needy families; her genuine compassion inspired me. **Thank you, Lord,** for everything that is beautiful and good in the world.

*F*ather, you've shown me that coveting isn't always as straightforward as wishing I had someone else's house or car. The covetous corruption that creeps in can wear any number of disguises, such as begrudging the fact that someone has been blessed in some way that I haven't. It can be despising someone else's success or hoping for their failure so I won't feel left behind. The list goes on, but the essence is my discontent with my own lot in life as I compare myself with someone else. **Set me free today** to enjoy the blessings you've provided without spoiling them by pointless comparisons.

Even so must their wives be grave,
not slanderers, sober, faithful in all things.

—1 Timothy 3:11

*F*or several years I've regularly met with a circle of women to play Bunco; I enjoy the camaraderie and the sense of community that the group provides. Membership has changed over the years. Some folks have moved away and new faces have joined up, and in many ways that's kept the group from stagnating. But recently, I've noticed that the dynamic of the group has changed in a not-so-positive way. While in the past, talk focused more on current events, movies, and books read, conversation has lately turned more than once to gossip. More distressing still, I've found myself drawn in, though afterwards, I invariably feel bad. Lord, please help me to stay faithful and clear minded. May I not be distracted by the strife that comes with gossip; please help me to redirect idle conversation into a more positive vein.

The God of my rock; in him will I trust: he is my shield, and the horn of my salvation, my high tower, and my refuge, my saviour; thou savest me from violence.

—2 Samuel 22:3

As I trust in you, God, I know you will fill my life with your hope. That hope will transcend into every area of my soul, and beautiful buds of joy and peace will begin to grow. I want your joy and peace to be obvious in my life. I'm tired of pretending to be joyful and acting like I'm peaceful. I desire those fruits to grow naturally, out of the wellspring of hope in my heart. Prod me to trust you at all times, Lord, and to rely on your Word. I know that my joy and peace are complete in you, and I have hope that you can work in me despite my weaknesses. I'm done with putting my hope into the changing tides of this world. I'm ready to put all of my hope in you, so real fruits of joy and peace can grow.

A new heart also will I give you, and a new spirit will I put within you: and I will take away the stony heart out of your flesh, and I will give you an heart of flesh.

—*Ezekiel 36:26*

*L*ord, bring me to the place where peace flows like a river, where soft green grasses gently hold the weight of my tired body, where the light of a new sunrise casts warmth.

*P*ressures in our lives can crowd out the joy. Let's remember to pray and ask God to help us **discover renewed joy.**

A soft answer turneth away wrath:
but grievous words stir up anger.

—*Proverbs 15:1*

My sister Emma and I are like night and day. Even though we grew up in the same house, and were raised by the same parents, our worldviews are strikingly different. We've had different ideas about how to help our aging parents, and we have different ideas on how to be a parent. And though we love each other, we don't always get along. Yesterday Emma criticized the way I'm handling a conflict with a mutual friend, and I had to bite my tongue to keep from lashing out. I managed to respond with a joke, and it was amazing how the tension between us drained away. God, help me to remember: when in a quarrel, I must strive to take the high road. A soft answer can defuse an argument **before** it begins.

Return unto thy rest, O my soul;
for the Lord hath dealt bountifully with thee.

—*Psalm 116:7*

*T*hank you, God, that even when I fret, I know without a doubt that you are using my unique, special gifts and talents to nurture and teach my children. When I get down on myself and am unsure of my abilities, remind me that your commitment to me is **lifelong**.

That I may publish with the voice of thanksgiving, and tell of all thy wondrous works.

—Psalm 26:7

As I follow in the children's wake as they discover bugs, plants, and cloud faces, your awesome creations bring us to our knees in daily thankfulness as we learn to name and know the works of your hands, Loving Creator.

*T*he prophet Isaiah wrote a number of inspired words from God that pointed to the coming of Christ to earth. He spoke of a great light shining on those living in a dark land. Spiritual darkness is the deepest kind of darkness. One may live in the darkness of being physically blind and yet have the light of Christ, which brings meaning, joy, and hope. Without the light of Christ in a life, there is something missing in the soul.

Commit thy way unto the Lord; trust also in him;
and he shall bring it to pass.

—Psalm 37:5

You call me to courage, Lord, but incrementally, as a child emboldened to walk along, placing each small foot in larger footprints. Following Father or Mother—as I am following you—knowing a path marked out this way—just step by step—but **you can only lead to safety.**

For every creature of God is good, and nothing to be refused, if it be received with thanksgiving.

—1 Timothy 4:4

Gratitude is an attitude of loving what you have, and this undoubtedly leads to having even more. When you open your eyes to the bountiful blessings already in your life, you realize just how **abundant the world really is.** Suddenly, you feel more giving, more loving, and more open to even greater blessings. Gratitude is a key that unlocks the door to treasures you already have, and it yields greater treasures yet to be discovered.

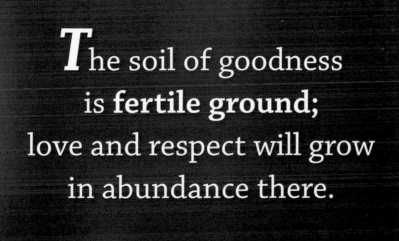

*T*he soil of goodness
is **fertile ground;**
love and respect will grow
in abundance there.

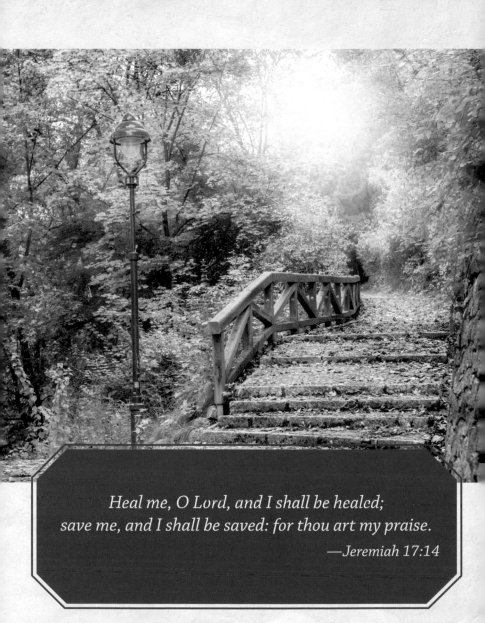

Heal me, O Lord, and I shall be healed;
save me, and I shall be saved: for thou art my praise.

—*Jeremiah 17:14*

*T*he healing presence of God is always working in and through us, but only when we give up the **illusion** of control.

And hope maketh not ashamed; because the love
of God is shed abroad in our hearts by the
Holy Ghost which is given unto us.

—Romans 5:5

*I*nstead of searching
for hope, **seek God.**
Hope will be your constant
companion when you do.

My Creator, **blessed is your presence.**
For you and you alone give me power to
walk through dark valleys into the light
again. You and you alone give me hope
when there seems to be no end to my suffering. You and you alone give me peace
when the noise of my life overwhelms
me. I ask that you give this same power,
hope, and peace to all who know discour-
agement, that they, too, may be emboldened and renewed by your everlasting
love. Amen.

*I sought the Lord, and he heard me,
and delivered me from all my fears.*

—*Psalm 34:4*

Calm me enough, O Lord, to breathe deeply and restoratively despite my racing heart, pounding headache, and generally fatigued body and mind. **Prayer restores me** in the presence of all that threatens to undo me, which I name to you now.

For I reckon that the sufferings of this present time are not worthy to be compared with the glory which shall be revealed in us.

—Romans 8:18

*D*ear God, hear my prayer. I am suffering and in need of your merciful blessings. Please take me into your arms. Give me the courage to keep going through difficult times and the fortitude to move beyond the outer illusions of pain and despair. **Only you can heal me, God.** In praise and thanks, amen.

Heal the sick, cleanse the lepers, raise the dead, cast out devils: freely ye have received, freely give.

—Matthew 10:8

An outstretched hand toward those in pain becomes a merciful extension of God's **healing touch.**

*I*t takes great courage to heal, Lord, great energy to reach out from this darkness to touch the hem of your garment and ask for healing. Bless the brave voices telling nightmare tales of dreadful wounds to the gifted healers of this world. Together, sufferers and healers are binding up damaged parts and laying down burdens carried so long.

He giveth power to the faint; and to them that have no might he increaseth strength.

—Isaiah 40:29

What a relief in this throwaway world of ever-changing values to know that you, O God, are the same yesterday, to-day, and tomorrow. Your trustworthiness and desire for all your children to have good things **never varies.** You are as sure as sunrise and sunset.

Although our eyes should always be turned toward God, sometimes we can do with a reminder of God's work just a little bit closer to home. **The faith of others** can serve as a reminder or an inspiration to strengthen our own faith. Just as we should provide encouragement to others, we can draw on others to help steady ourselves.

O Lord my God, I cried unto thee, and thou hast healed me. O Lord, thou hast brought up my soul from the grave: thou hast kept me alive, that I should not go down to the pit.

—*Psalm 30:2–3*

God, bless this situation with the gentle, healing power of your love, that I may find the courage to carry on through this dark time of loss and the grace to believe there is **happiness ahead.** Amen.

*D*ear Lord, thank you for healing my heart and bringing joy and meaning back into my life. Thank you for the people who truly care for me. Help me be a soothing and joyful presence in their lives as well. Amen.

Therefore I say unto you, Take no thought for your life, what ye shall eat, or what ye shall drink; nor yet for your body, what ye shall put on. Is not the life more than meat, and the body than raiment?

—Matthew 6:25

I recently graduated from college, and while I look for a job in my field of study, which is geology, I've been working a series of lower-paying jobs to pay the bills. I have managed to create a life I'm proud of. I pride myself on being independent and not living beyond my means. But my student loan debt is substantial, and there are not too many miles left on the old car I've been driving since high school. My current jobs do not offer health insurance. Some days I feel discouraged that I have not yet found the work for which my education has prepared me. Some nights I can't sleep for worrying about finances, or what expenses lie around the corner. God, help me to remember that you are there: to support me, and imbue me with strength and wisdom. **Help me to remember that you will provide.**

Beareth all things, believeth all things,
hopeth all things, endureth all things.

—1 Corinthians 13:7

*H*eavenly Father, you say that you will heal me. Please help me realize there are different forms of healing. While your healing is sometimes miraculous and other times almost common and everyday, your healing is on occasion invisible. There are moments when life doesn't seem to change, and I have to look inside to find a place of acceptance. It is in this place where I am reminded that who I am is separate from the pain that invades my life. **Please help me to turn my thoughts to you.** Amen.

*F*aith sometimes means **giving back** to God the things and people we cherish most. Abraham's faith was tested, and his response has become a model of faith for all believers.

Now faith is the substance of things hoped for, the evidence of things not seen.

—*Hebrews 11:1*

Dear Lord, I am feeling more hopeful these days. For a while, I forgot to include your loving guidance and grace in my life. I forgot that if I pray and meditate and just get silent enough to listen, you always give me the answers I seek and the direction I need to overcome anything life hands me. I pray for continued guidance and wisdom, and that I may always live from a place of hope instead of fear, and a place of possibilities instead of limitations. You are my wings and my rock, allowing me to both soar higher and stay grounded. No matter what I may be facing, staying in the comforting light of your presence gives me the hope I need to carry on with my head held high and my heart strong and fearless. Thank you for the **gift of hope**. Amen.

*H*uman faith lives between two extremes, Lord: **It's neither completely blind nor able to see everything.** It has plenty of evidence when it steps out and trusts you, but it takes each step with a good many questions still unanswered. It's really quite an adventure, this life of faith. And Lord, I must confess that experiencing your faithfulness over time makes it easier and easier to trust you with the unknown in life. Thank you for your unshakable devotion.

Charity suffereth long, and is kind; charity envieth not; charity vaunteth not itself, is not puffed up.

—*1 Corinthians 13:4*

Countless books and movies have been dedicated to the idea of love. Ah, love! In many stories, love is romantic, heedless, and, tellingly, "I"-based. Am I the object of affection? And yet God teaches us that love (or as it is referred to in the King James Version of the Bible, charity), is a two-way exchange of something much more profound: its very nature is selfless and humble. Love isn't, in fact, the flash and show; it's a grounded exchange, a deep, mutual caring and respect that endures long after the first brilliant connection. God reminds us that **true love** goes beyond that initial glitz and flurry; when we know true love, he counsels, we feel no need to flaunt it.

Thou shalt not avenge, nor bear any grudge against the children of thy people, but thou shalt love thy neighbour as thyself: I am the Lord.

—*Leviticus 19:18*

God's love does not draw lines. It comes with open eyes, open arms, and an open heart. Can we take the risk of **loving our neighbor** with God's kind of love?

*T*wo people in love is a **work of art**—
a masterpiece sublime. Two equal halves
that make a whole—an image so divine.

Her children arise up, and call her blessed;
her husband also, and he praiseth her.

—*Proverbs 31:28*

*T*his morning there were, as my grandfather used to say, a lot of moving parts. My husband needed to catch an early train into the city, my son, Ben, couldn't find his chemistry textbook, and our dog scarfed down the bread I'd intended for everyone's lunch sandwiches. I was feeling pretty frazzled, and had to get to work myself. But after the boys got out the door and I'd made sure the dog was none the worse for wear, I took a deep breath and noticed that Ben had made me a pot of coffee before leaving for school. My husband had promised he'd order us a pizza tonight so that no one had to cook. And our dog? Well, it's hard to stay mad at a smiling dog! Lord, even when things are a little crazy around our house, I thank you: **I am blessed by my family.**

For I am persuaded, that neither death, nor life,
nor angels, nor principalities, nor powers, nor things
present, nor things to come, nor height, nor depth, nor
any other creature, shall be able to separate
us from the love of God, which is in
Christ Jesus our Lord.

—Romans 8:38–39

*T*hank you, my love, for trusting me enough to tear down walls of fear and doubt. Thank you for opening wide the door of your wounded heart to let me love you.

And thou shalt love the Lord thy God with all thine heart, and with all thy soul, and with all thy might.

—*Deuteronomy 6:5*

God wants us to love him, not because he is greedy for love, but because when we are devoted to loving him, we get in touch with his powerful, everlasting love for us. When we do, we cannot contain it, and it overflows to others.

God's desire for love from us is not primarily for his benefit, **but for ours.** One of his deepest desires is that we know his love, and somehow when we take action to love him, it is then we discover just how much he loves us.

Be not deceived: evil communications
corrupt good manners.

—1 Corinthians 15:33

I appreciate the connections made possible by social media, but I also recognize that like everything else, when it comes to technology, **moderation is key.** Yesterday I was glued to a series of screens throughout the day, from phone to laptop, and when I tore myself away to make dinner, I found myself in a particularly ill humor. While I had happily corresponded with an old friend who lives on another continent, I'd also witnessed a good deal of negativity, judgmental attitudes, and blatantly hateful behavior online. The prolonged exposure had soured my spirit, and when I snapped at my son, I realized that my choices that day did not benefit my family or me. God, help me to capitalize on the good inherent in technology, while also practicing moderation and sound judgment. Do not let me fall prey to the negativity that can be part of the online experience.

My mouth shall speak of wisdom; and the meditation of my heart shall be of understanding.

—Psalm 49:3

*L*ord, I can hear your voice in the bubbling brook, see your beauty in the petals of a flower, and feel your gentleness in the evening breeze and in the soft kiss of a child. **Thank you** for all of these gifts.

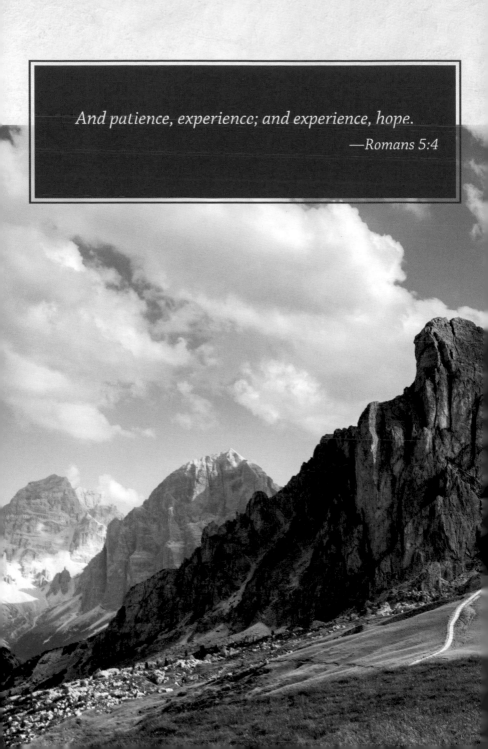

And patience, experience; and experience, hope.

—Romans 5:4

*T*hroughout life, one of the hardest words to hear is WAIT. Sometimes we may anxiously wonder, "Where is God when I need him?" Patience is developed through faithful waiting. God has a design in even the most difficult situations that will enable our character to become stronger. As we learn patience, we also learn to trust that God has our best interests in mind. He cannot abandon us, and he will always rescue us **at just the right time.**

These things I have spoken unto you,
that in me ye might have peace.
In the world ye shall have tribulation:
but be of good cheer; I have overcome the world.

—John 16:33

*T*he sunshine of your caring gaze, the water of your gentle words, the nourishment of your tender touch have revived this limp flower called my soul. I am once again in full bloom **because of your love.**

And the work of righteousness shall be peace;
and the effect of righteousness quietness and
assurance for ever.

—Isaiah 32:17

*L*ove is never noisy, obvious, or demanding. It is the gentle whisper of the heart, the soft lullaby of the **soul**.

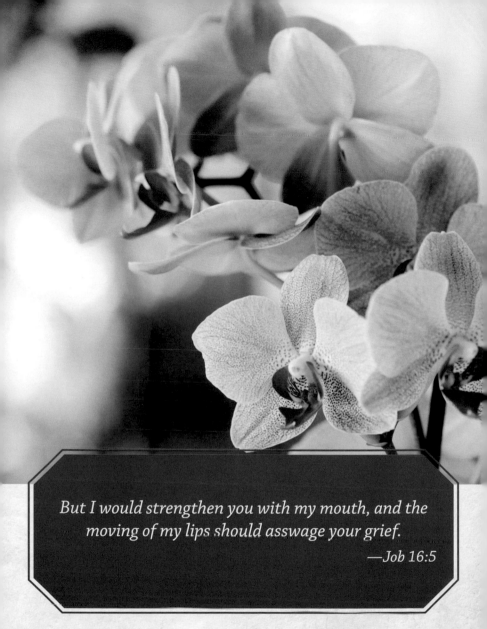

But I would strengthen you with my mouth, and the moving of my lips should asswage your grief.

—*Job 16:5*

One of my oldest friends, Beth, recently and unexpectedly lost her husband. Dan was killed in a freak car accident, and Beth and her children have been blindsided by the loss. I have spent a lot of time with the family since the accident, and see how even the most well-meaning people have sometimes said hurtful things to Beth in their efforts to show concern. I want to avoid causing my friend any more pain, and so for the most part have tried to provide solace with my quiet presence. But I know that the right words can assuage grief. Dear Lord, grant me the wisdom to comfort my friends in their time of need. Help me to know what to say.

She is more precious than rubies: and all the things thou canst desire are not to be compared unto her.

—Proverbs 3:15

*L*ife can be complicated; in the larger world we are challenged, sometimes on a daily basis, to be our best selves. Perhaps we don't see eye-to-eye with a coworker. Maybe we need to have a talk with a friend who has hurt us, even though we dislike confrontation. Can it be that the sweet, adoring toddler we walked to pre-school seemingly yesterday has morphed into a teen who is trying to individuate—but doesn't yet know how to do that in a mature or loving way? Though life's hurts can chip away at our spirits, God reminds us that each of us has value. May we never lose sight of the fact that God created us! May we never lose sight of our inherent worth.

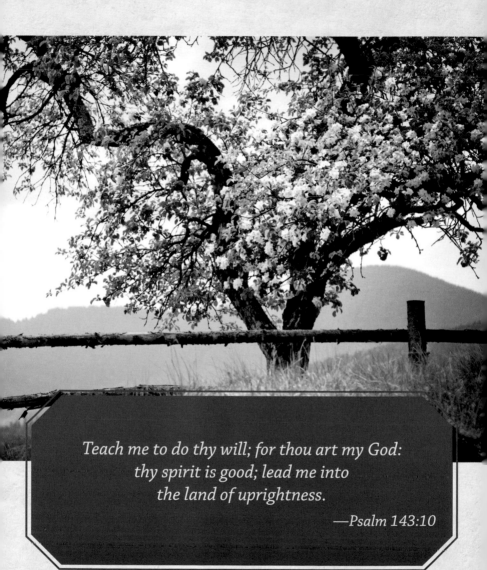

Teach me to do thy will; for thou art my God:
thy spirit is good; lead me into
the land of uprightness.

—*Psalm 143:10*

As my husband and children go out into the world, it is comforting to know that the Lord **goes before them** to lead the way and to give them light.

Great peace have they which love thy law:
and nothing shall offend them.

—*Psalm 119:165*

*F*ear and lack of understanding can prevent us from loving our neighbor. If we pray for his assistance, God will help us reach out to our neighbor with his love.

When neighbors don't measure up to our expectations, we can go to God for a **change of heart.** With his example and assistance, we can love our neighbors as God wants us to.

Strength and honour are her clothing; and she shall rejoice in time to come. She openeth her mouth with wisdom; and in her tongue is the law of kindness.

—*Proverbs 31:25–26*

Some chapters in life are more difficult than others. My mother—who has been a confidante, a support, and a role model my entire life—was recently diagnosed with dementia. Dementia is a long good-bye, and even as I grieve this loss and help her navigate a very scary new chapter, I am determined to remain present for my husband and our two children. Some days, I struggle against feeling ground down and bitter. Many days, I am angry that this disease is robbing me of my wise mother, and my children of the grandmother they have known. God, I am afraid. Please help me to remain steadfast and honorable in my actions, no matter what turns life takes in the days ahead.

> *Thou art all fair, my love; there is no spot in thee.*
>
> —*Psalm 37:5*

*I*t is challenging to be a woman growing up in today's society. Media bombards us with images that define beauty along a narrow spectrum. And though many of the photos we see—online, in magazines, and on television—are unrealistic versions of feminine beauty (some have even been altered), we are led to believe that unless we look a certain way, we are not beautiful. As the mother of two daughters, I am dedicated to combatting this insidious message; my goal is to help my girls feel good about themselves and their bodies. I try to model healthy habits: a balanced diet, regular exercise, and a positive attitude about the strong, healthy body God has granted me. I try to demonstrate, through my actions, the importance of being a decent person. God, help me to remember—and instill in my daughters—that beauty comes in many forms, especially from **within.**

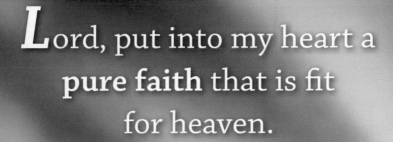

*L*ord, put into my heart a
pure faith that is fit
for heaven.

Finally, brethren, farewell. Be perfect, be of good comfort, be of one mind, live in peace; and the God of love and peace shall be with you.

—1 Corinthians 13:11

*T*hough we may not choose our family members, we eventually come to the understanding that someone far wiser chose them for us. Each family member has something special to teach us, whether it be forgiveness, tolerance, or acceptance. Some members give us nothing but love. Some give us nothing but grief. It is the former we often embrace, yet it is the latter from which we have **the most to learn.**

She is like the merchants' ships;
she bringeth her food from afar.

—Proverbs 31:14

*T*he recession hit our family hard, but I'm proud of the way my husband and I stepped up and managed what could have been a scary situation. I've worked outside the home since our children were small, but after the market collapse, my husband was laid off and we both took on a series of extra jobs to make ends meet. It wasn't always easy, but together, we have stayed on top of the bills and kept things stable for the kids. I see the same grit in my sister, who is a young widow with a son of her own. **"Women are strong,"** I tell her, and I mean it. Dear Lord, thank you for this strength. Women are providers!

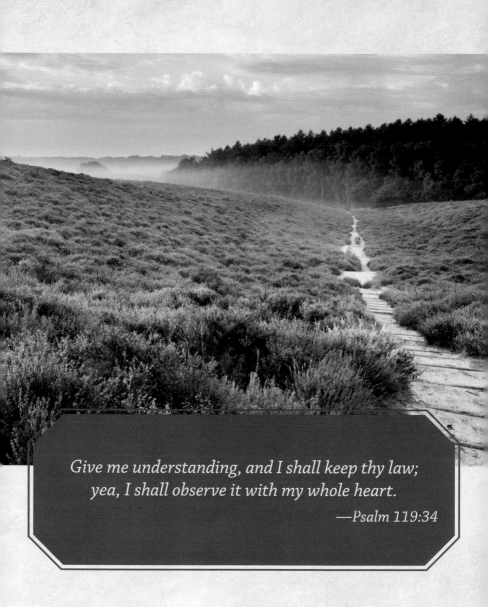

Give me understanding, and I shall keep thy law;
yea, I shall observe it with my whole heart.

—*Psalm 119:34*

*F*ather God, we know that to receive the blessing of healing, **the heart must be open.** But when we are mad, we close off the heart as if it were a prison. Remind us that a heart that is shut cannot receive understanding, acceptance, and renewal. Even though we feel angry, we must keep the heart's door slightly ajar so your grace can enter and fill our darkness with the light of hope.

And blessed is she that believed: for there shall be a performance of those things which were told her from the Lord.

—Luke 1:45

Our relationships strengthen us. This came home to me the other day, when an exchange with a coworker left me feeling irresolute and unsettled. During my commute home, my stomach was in knots. I went over and over the disagreement in my head. It was hard to sort out whether I'd handled things with grace. When I got home, I found that my husband had started dinner; the warm atmosphere of love and regard unclenched my heart, and I was able to talk frankly about the day. My husband's nonjudgmental but clear-sighted perspective helped me sort how to remedy the situation. After we talked, we took a moment to pray together. God, thank you for reminding us of the importance of believing in you and in one another.

Or let him take hold of my strength,
that he may make peace with me;
and he shall make peace with me.

—Isaiah 27:5

As the seasons change and the exterior world becomes a different place, we can find the courage and power and guidance we need by **staying focused** on the unchangeable, unmovable, infinite center within.

*But whoso hearkeneth unto me shall dwell safely,
and shall be quiet from fear of evil.*

—*Proverbs 1:33*

226

God, when life feels like a ride that won't let us off, remind us that you are waiting for us to reach up to you. And when we finally do, thank you for being there to lift us to peace and safety.

*I*n God's arms is the only place of **true safety.**

I will both lay me down in peace, and sleep: for thou, Lord, only makest me dwell in safety.

—Psalm 4:8

*P*recious Lord, bless me with your grace that I may experience the deepest peace and healing only you can provide. Show me the merciful love that knows no end so I may rest today knowing **I am cared for.** Amen.

God is faithful, by whom ye were called unto the fellowship of his Son Jesus Christ our Lord.

—*1 Corinthians 1:9*

*L*ast year, an old college friend called with the devastating news that after twenty-three years of marriage, her husband had admitted to a longstanding affair and asked for a divorce. My friend had felt secure in her husband's love and was blindsided by this betrayal. In the months since, she has taken comfort in the community of her church, and found solace in her faith. "It's true that sometimes people disappoint us," she told me recently. We'd met for lunch, and though she spoke wryly, she looked and sounded better than she had in months. "But God is always faithful to us." I was struck by her words, and on the walk home pondered the resilience that grows when we know someone has our back. Dear Lord, help me to remember that you are a constant in my life, **in times of joy but also adversity.**

*And now abideth faith, hope, charity, these three;
but the greatest of these is charity.*

—*1 Corinthians 13:13*

*I*t's amazing how the little things—
like your smile—can lift my spirits and
remind me I am loved.

These things have I spoken unto you, that my joy might remain in you, and that your joy might be full.

—*John 15:11*

Young children have a particularly deep capacity for joy. They love fiercely and play hard; their worldview is often one of opportunity and abundance. As we grow, experiences good and bad accrue. We take on more responsibility, for others and for ourselves, and can lose sight of that deep well of joy. It's still there, if we are mindful. But joy is tricky in that it can manifest itself in opposites: there is joy in community, even as it exists in solitary pursuits. A gorgeous summer sky brings joy, as does a brooding landscape. Sometimes we don't recognize joy, but it is there: we can still access it, whether it feels like good loneliness, hilarity, or a deep stillness. It is a gift we must not lose sight of. Dear Lord, thank you for joy, which comes from you.

But the fruit of the Spirit is love, joy, peace, longsuffering, gentleness, goodness, faith, meekness, temperance: against such there is no law.

—Galatians 5:22–23

*I*t is only through the eyes
of someone we love that
we see who we really are.

But if we hope for that we see not,
then do we with patience wait for it.

—*Romans 8:25*

*T*each us to know, God, that it is exactly at the point of our deepest despair that you are closest. For at those times we can finally admit we have wandered in the dark, without a clue. Yet you have been there with us all along. Thank you for your abiding presence.

For all the law is fulfilled in one word, even in this;
Thou shalt love thy neighbour as thyself.

—*Galatians 5:14*

Stand in a beloved's shade, not shadow, and discover new sights to share, new directions to go, all leading to even more reasons for **standing together.**

I will speak of the glorious honour of thy majesty, and of thy wondrous works.

—*Psalm 145:5*

*I*t's easy to praise you for your majesty and power when we see thundering waterfalls, crashing ocean waves, or majestic sunsets. Help us **learn to praise you** when we see a dewdrop, a seedling, or an ant.

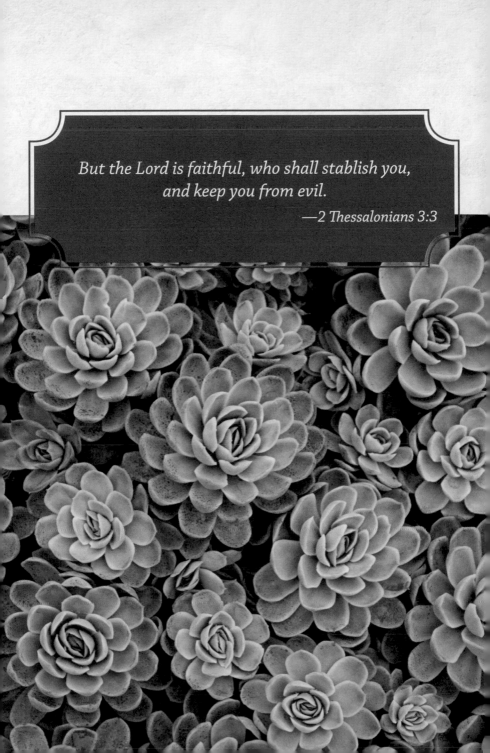

But the Lord is faithful, who shall stablish you,
and keep you from evil.

—2 Thessalonians 3:3

God of all comfort, I know that with you by my side **I am never alone.** Your perfect love casts out all fear, doubt, and uncertainty. Your presence emboldens and empowers me. You are the light that leads me to safety again. Amen.

To the only wise God our Saviour,
be glory and majesty, dominion and power,
both now and ever. Amen.

—Jude 1:25

When we shift our focus beyond the physical, we realize we exist amidst a presence and power that is **transcendent.**

And be not conformed to this world:
but be ye transformed by the renewing of your mind,
that ye may prove what is that good, and acceptable,
and perfect, will of God.

—*Romans 12:2*

As the mother of a young child, I naturally cross paths with other moms—some work outside the home, and some are stay-at-home moms, like me. At this time of my life, staying home with my baby is the right choice for our family, but I respect those who make a different choice. I have been surprised and disappointed at how vehemently mothers on both sides of the home-or-work question have criticized what they see as the "incorrect" path. My best girlfriend, a mom of two, works full-time, and both of us have encountered criticisms from those who make claims about who we are as people based on our choice in this matter. It can be hard not to become defensive, and my friend feels the same. Lord, help us to be unconcerned when the world tries to define us. Help us to access strength and our best selves through spirituality.

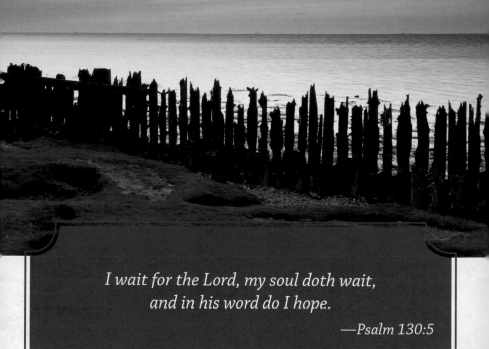

*I wait for the Lord, my soul doth wait,
and in his word do I hope.*

—*Psalm 130:5*

I asked for God's greatest riches, and he gave me **contentment.**

Thou art my hiding place and my shield:
I hope in thy word.

—*Psalm 119:116*

*S*tep into the future with faith in your ability to **conquer the unknown.**

When we shift our focus beyond the physical, we realize we exist amidst a presence and power that is **transcendent.**